Written by **Sammy Jordan**
Illustrated by **Sarah Joy Marshall**

GOD'S BIG STORY

Printed in the United Kingdom
First Printing, 2020

ISBN: 978-1-9163091-0-4 (Paperback)

Sammy Jordan Publishing
Southampton
SO16 3PZ

Do you know something BIG?

What makes something BIG?

Some things are BIG in size
... tall towers, tall people,
rollercoasters, elephants,
giraffes and even the sky.

Some things are BIG because
they are important ... kings and
queens, prime ministers and
presidents ...and presents!

Some things are BIG because
they are exciting ... like holidays,
birthdays and Christmas.

Can you think of more BIG things?

GOD'S BIG STORY

What about stories?

Can stories be BIG?

Stories are BIG if they are about BIG characters.

Stories are BIG if they are about important things, or if they are BIG on excitement.

Sometimes stories are just BIG in size.

Do you know any BIG stories?

The story you are about to read is a BIG story.

In fact, it's THE BIG story.

Stories usually have a beginning,
a middle and an end and
God's BIG story does too.

The beginning is when God made
everything – the whole of creation!

Wow!

That's a lot of things ...

Animals and birds, plants and trees,
the sky and sea, mountains and
valleys, beaches and waves, snow
and thunder, sunshine ... and rain!

Oh ... and people too!

**How many more things that
God made can you think of?**

Have you ever made something?

Were you pleased with it?

The world God made was perfect and He loved it. God looked at His creation and said it was "Good!"

What's your favourite part of creation?

God loved people and wanted to be friends with them.

God still loves people and wants to be friends.

Who are your friends?

Is God your friend?

5

Choices ...

**Chocolate or strawberry
ice cream?**

**Cheese and tomato or
pepperoni pizza?**

**Salt n' vinegar or cheese
and onion crisps?**

What choices do you make?

God gave people a choice.

God gave people a choice
because He loves them.

God gave people a choice about
whether to be His friends ... or not.

People chose 'not'.

**Have you ever fallen
out with a friend?**

How did you 'make friends' again?

People chose to walk away
from God and not be friends.

The world wasn't perfect anymore.

It was BROKEN.

We can see how BROKEN it is when we look around us ... when people fight or go to war, when people get sick or are poor, when we argue and don't share, when we are greedy and unkind.

Can you think of any other examples of how the world is broken?

Have you ever broken anything?

What did you do?

How do you fix broken things?

The broken world can't be fixed with glue, sticky tape ... or even a hug.

The broken world needs to be fixed with love and a special 'Sorry'.

People tried to fix the broken world, but they tried to fix it without God's help.

Have you ever tried to play a game without following the instructions?

What happened?

People's attempts to fix the broken world on their own, didn't work either.

God tried to help.

God sent His messengers with instructions to show people how to be friends with Him again.

People like Moses, Samuel, David, Jonah and Nehemiah; you might have heard of some of them.

Can you think of any more of God's messengers?

But the world was too broken. People were too broken. God's messages and instructions didn't get through.

But God had a plan ...

God always had a plan!

God's plan was Jesus.

God sent His Son Jesus to fix the broken world and help people be friends with God again.

Jesus' life showed people what God is like.

Do you celebrate Jesus' birth at Christmas?

Do you know any of the stories about Jesus' life?

Perhaps you can spot a few clues in the pictures on this page.

What happens when you do something wrong, perhaps at home or school?

Wrong often leads to a punishment, this is a consequence; something that happens because of a wrong thing.

It's the same with God.

The consequence of peoples' wrong choices was a broken world and a broken friendship with God.

Jesus had never done anything wrong but died on a cross to sort the consequences of people's wrong choices.

Christians call this Good Friday. It's called 'Good' because it's good for people.

Jesus died because He loves people. He took the punishment so people can be forgiven for wrong choices and can be friends with God again.

Jesus came back to life showing the consequences of people's wrong choices have been sorted.

This is what Christians celebrate at Easter.

Now, God and people can be friends again ... we just need to say sorry!

What job would you like
when you are older?

**A teacher? Nurse? Police Officer?
Chef? Engineer? Inventor?**

Perhaps you can think of more?

When you become Jesus' friend,
He gives you a job straight away!

Jesus wants His friends to
love him, to love people
and to love the world.

**Do you think this is a
job you could do?**

When Jesus' friends do this,
slowly, ever so slowly … what was
broken will begin to be fixed.

People will begin to see what
God is like, that God loves people
and the world He made.

We're still in the middle of the story now. The world is still broken,

But

One day the world WILL be completely fixed — it will be like new.

One day Jesus WILL come back to earth and the world WON'T be broken anymore.

It's a bit like a game where you know which team is going to win because they can't lose; but there is still time to play.

Who helps you?

Hopefully there are lots of people who help you.

Teachers help you at school.

Doctors help you if you get sick.

Friends help you if you are lonely or want to play.

Parents help you ... with just about anything!

Can you think of anyone else?

Having a job when you are young might seem scary.

Don't be scared.

God has sent His special helper to help you do the job He needs you to do.

God's special helper is called the Holy Spirit. The Holy Spirit helps people to live for Jesus.

A bit like batteries, the Holy Spirit gives people the power to live for Jesus.

The Holy Spirit helps people to love Jesus, each other and the world.

Do you need the Holy Spirit to help you?

What do you think a perfect world would be like?

One day Jesus will return.

Not as a baby at Christmas, but as King of the whole world.

The end of our BIG story hasn't happened .... yet!

When Jesus comes back, the broken world will be completely fixed because Jesus took the consequences for wrong choices when He died on the cross.

When Jesus came back to life it showed that the consequences of wrong choices had been sorted forever.

So, the end of the story has already been written.

But the world still looks broken, doesn't it?

People still make wrong choices and we see the consequences all around us.

We might know the end of the story but we're still in the middle of it.

Jesus promised that one day, He will come again, and when He does, the world will be made perfect again.

No more broken world!

No more consequences for wrong choices!

No more wrong choices!

People will be friends with God and live with him in a perfect world ... forever!

Now that's what I call a BIG story!

Some BIG stories are exciting and made up.

This BIG story is true.

I wonder if you want to be Jesus' friend?

I wonder if you want to say sorry for the wrong choices you make?

I wonder if you want the job of helping God to fix the broken world?

If you do, you might want to say this prayer.

Please tell a grown up so that they can help you.

Dear Jesus,

I'm sorry for the wrong choices I've made.

I'm sorry that the world is broken and not how you want it to be.

Thank you that you dealt with the consequences of my wrong choices when you died for me.

Thank you that you love me.

I want to be your friend.

Please help me to live for you. I want to help fix the broken world.

Please help me with the power of your Holy Spirit.

Amen

Lightning Source UK Ltd.
Milton Keynes UK
UKRC031133090322
399804UK00001B/1